beginnings

longing to belong

Participant's Guide

Andy Langford, Mark Ralls,
and Rob Weber

Abingdon Press / Nashville

Beginnings: Longing to Belong
Participant's Guide

Copyright © 2008 by Abingdon Press.

Scripture (unless otherwise indicated) taken from the Holy Bible, Today's New International® Version TNIV©. Copyright 2001, 2005 by International Bible Society®. Used by permission of International Bible Society®. All rights reserved worldwide. "TNIV" and "Today's New International Version" are trademarks registered in the United States Patent and Trademark Office by International Bible Society®.

This book is printed on acid-free, elemental chlorine–free paper.

ISBN 978-0-687-33596-1

08 09 10 11 12 13 14 15 16 17— 10 9 8 7 6 5 4 3 2 1

MANUFACTURED IN THE UNITED STATES OF AMERICA

Contents

Welcome!

Welcome to *Beginnings: Longing to Belong*, a ten-session program in Christian community building. We believe these next few weeks could be very important for you. Each week you will gather with a group of friends to consider how you can go deeper in your relationship with God and with other followers of Jesus Christ. You will explore who you are, who God is, and how our lives intersect with God and fellow disciples of our Savior.

Each week you will watch a short presentation by Rob Weber exploring a different aspect of Christian community. There is no need to take notes, as if these talks were formal lectures. Instead, we encourage you to write down your reflections and comments that the presentation calls to your mind. Each presentation is provocative, intended to encourage you to engage with the issues Rob will introduce.

Everyone will then gather in a small group for discussion. You are also invited to read the companion book, *Around the Fire: A Participant's Companion,* for further exploration of the weekly topics. Each chapter will provide you with a fuller understanding of the theme discussed in Rob's video, how the theme connects to the Christian faith, and some ways you can begin to incorporate the habit of community building into your life.

This book accompanies the ten sessions of *Beginnings: Longing to Belong*. It provides several ways to respond to what you have heard in the lectures:

Scripture Passage provides the basis for each presentation along with space for you to write out your reflections and comments.

Signs of God's Presence are a variety of objects that remind us of different aspects of the community of Christ.

Group Questions will spark discussions in your small group. These questions will help you engage what you have just heard and prepare you for your reading and reflection in the week ahead.

Group Exercise allows you to experiment with each new aspect of living in community with other followers of Jesus Christ. This exercise may open new, unexpected avenues of thought or allow you to experience what it feels like to "live out" being in community with others.

Weekly Reflection provides ideas for you to consider throughout the week. This personal reflection will help you see each aspect of the body of Christ in a new way.

We hope that this Participant's Guide, along with every part of *Beginnings: Longing to Belong,* enriches your experience of being a part of the body of Christ.

Scriptural Foundation

The central biblical narrative that lays the foundation for *Longing to Belong* comes from the fifth book in the New Testament: the Acts of the Apostles. In response to the gift of the Holy Spirit on the Day of Pentecost, the original followers of Jesus Christ formed the first community of Christians; they organized themselves as the living body of Christ. *Longing to Belong* uses this passage of Scripture as our starting point:

So those people in Jerusalem who welcomed Simon Peter's message about Jesus Christ were baptized, and on that day of Pentecost about three thousand persons became followers of Jesus Christ. All of these followers of Jesus Christ devoted themselves to the first disciples' teaching and fellowship, the holy meal of bread and cup, and prayer. Everyone was filled with awe, and many wonders and miracles were accomplished.

All who believed lived in close fellowship and possessed all things in common. They sold their belongings and property and gave their money to anyone who had need. Day by day, the followers of Jesus Christ spent much time together in the temple in Jerusalem. They shared meals together from home to home. They ate their food with joy and thanksgiving, praising God and showing kindness to everyone. And day by day, the Lord God increased the number of persons who were being saved.

(Acts 2:41-47, authors' paraphrase)

1.
Longing to Belong?

Introduction

Scripture Passage

In my former book [The Gospel According to Luke], Theophilus [lover of God], I wrote about all that Jesus began to do and to teach until the day he was taken up to heaven, after giving instructions through the Holy Spirit to the apostles he had chosen. After his suffering, he presented himself to them and gave many convincing proofs that he was alive. He appeared to them over a period of forty days and spoke about the kingdom of God. On one occasion, while he was eating with them, he gave them this command: "Do not leave Jerusalem, but wait for the gift my Father promised, which you have heard me speak about. For John baptized with water, but in a few days you will be baptized with the Holy Spirit. . . .

"You will receive power when the Holy Spirit comes on you; and you will be my witnesses in Jerusalem, and in all Judea and Samaria, and to the end of the earth."

After he said this, he was taken up before their very eyes, and a cloud hid him from their sight. . . .

When the day of Pentecost came, they [the apostles] were all together in one place. Suddenly a sound like the blowing of a violent wind came from heaven and filled the whole house where they were sitting. They saw what seemed to be tongues of fire that separated and came to rest on each of them. All of them were filled with the Holy Spirit and began to speak in other tongues as the Spirit enabled them.

Now there were staying in Jerusalem God-fearing Jews from every nation under heaven. When they heard this sound, a crowd came together in bewilderment, because each one heard their own language being spoken. . . .

When the people heard this, they were cut to the heart and said to Peter and the other apostles, "Brothers, what shall we do?"

Peter replied, "Repent and be baptized...."

Those who accepted his message were baptized, and about three thousand were added to their number that day. (Acts 1:1-9; 2:1-41, excerpts)

Reflections and Comments

_____
_____
_____
_____
_____
_____
_____
_____
_____
_____
_____
_____
_____
_____
_____
_____
_____
_____
_____
_____
_____
_____

Sign of God's Presence

Lighted candle, as a sign of the Holy Spirit at Pentecost

Group Questions

1. Think of a classic television show in which the characters were part of a community that seemed attractive to you, such as *Cheers, Friends, The*

Andy Griffith Show, or *Star Trek.* Name the show and describe why the characters represent a supportive community.

2. Like Rob's experience in joining a band, as described in the video, have you found community in unexpected places? Share a time in your life when you were a new kid on the block, a new person at the office, or a new member of a congregation. How long did it take to feel part of that group? What helped make it happen? Who welcomed you into that community? How did they do so?

3. Rob describes the early church as a different kind of congregation from those most of us experience today. When someone says the word *church,* what images come to your mind? What draws you into this community? What causes you concern?

Group Exercise

For two minutes, focus on the lighted candle and flame. In silence, reflect on why you are participating in this small group. Your leader will end this time of silence with a final prayer for your whole group.

Weekly Reflection

Read the text of Acts 2:41-47 (found on page 7). Reflect on the characteristics of the new reality being experienced by those present on the Day of Pentecost. Think of the community that is being formed in your small group. What do you hope will happen in this new community? What do you hope to share with your fellow participants?

_____

_____

_____

_____

_____

_____

_____

_____

_____

_____

_____

_____

_____

_____

_____

* * *

For further exploration, we invite you to read Chapter 1 in *Around the Fire*. The chapter discusses our spiritual isolation and compares it with the feelings of the first disciples immediately after Jesus' ascension into heaven. The Holy Spirit responds to our feeling that we are lost and begins to bring us into community with each other. All of us need to have a place where everybody knows our name. The feeling of interconnectedness is expressed in the African word *ubuntu*.

2.

How Do We Find Our Place?

Baptism

Scripture Passage

So those people in Jerusalem who welcomed Simon Peter's message about
Jesus Christ were baptized, and on that day of Pentecost about three thousand
persons became followers of Jesus Christ. All of these followers of Jesus
Christ devoted themselves to the first disciples' teaching and fellowship.

(Acts 2:41-42a, authors' paraphrase)

Reflections and Comments

_____
_____
_____
_____
_____
_____
_____
_____
_____
_____
_____
_____
_____
_____
_____
_____
_____
_____
_____
_____

Signs of God's Presence

When you gather as a group, focus briefly on the lighted candle. Then focus on the small bowl of water, as a sign of baptism. Your leader may also have shower hooks that say, "I am baptized" or "I am a child of God." If you receive such a gift, place it in your shower or bathtub to help you remember your baptism.

Group Questions

1. Rob describes himself as a son, husband, father, and pastor. With which words do you describe yourself? Which description did you say first? Why did that answer immediately come to mind? Is it truly the one you cherish most?

2. If you have been baptized, describe your baptism. If you are able, can you tell the others what happened? Where did it take place? How old were you? Who was there? Can you describe any difference that your baptism has made in your life? If you have not been baptized, describe another experience in which you were initiated into a group or community. In the movie *The Lion King*, Simba looks into the water and remembers who he is. How might baptism or an initiation help you remember who you are?

3. Imagine your congregation as a group of persons at a community dance. Where do you picture yourself in the dance: sitting alone and off to the side, taking a few first steps, beginning to catch the rhythm, right in the middle of the action, or exhausted and ready to take a break? Does this picture express where you are or where you would like to be?

Group Exercise

Take ten minutes for your small group to create a covenant or agreement that will bind you together over the next nine weeks. What are your expectations of one another? Some possible answers include: attend each week, pray for your group, listen carefully when another person speaks, and keep stories and information confidential. Have someone write the group's answers on a sheet of paper. Do not be too legalistic, too anxious about exact language, or too exhaustive in making the list. Bring the resulting covenant to the session each week to remind one another of your mutual expectations.

Place the bowl of water before you. Touch the water with your fingers. Touch your wet fingers to your forehead or your heart, or make the sign of the cross across your chest. As you do so, say aloud, "I am baptized." If you have not been baptized, just gaze upon the water. Pass the bowl of water to the next person in your group.

Weekly Reflection

Throughout the upcoming week, whenever you take a shower or bath, splash water on your face and say aloud, "I am baptized."

Reflect on the web of relationships in which you find yourself and on the amount of time you will give to each of these relationships in the coming week. Which of the relationships are especially important to you? To which do you need to devote more attention? To which do you need to devote less attention?

_____

_____

_____

_____

_____

_____

_____

_____

_____

_____

_____

_____

_____

* * *

For further exploration, we invite you to read Chapter 2 in *Around the Fire*. The chapter examines the baptismal practices of the early church and ways in which our use of water may remind us that all of us are children of God. In the chapter we are asked to remember our own baptism and celebrate how the water and Holy Spirit have brought us into communion with other Christians. A scene from the movie *Tender Mercies* is described to illustrate this truth.

3.

What Are We Hungry For?

Holy Communion

Scripture Passages

They devoted themselves to ... the holy meal of bread and cup.
(Acts 2:42a & b, authors' paraphrase)

So whether you eat or drink or whatever you do, do it all for the glory of God. (1 Corinthians 10:31)

Reflections and Comments

_____
_____
_____
_____
_____
_____
_____
_____
_____
_____
_____
_____
_____
_____
_____
_____
_____
_____
_____

Signs of God's Presence

When you gather as a group, focus briefly on the lighted candle and touch the baptismal water in the bowl. Review your covenant agreement. Then focus on the loaf of bread and the cup of wine or grape juice, as signs of Holy Communion.

Group Questions

1. In the video, Rob recalls meals at his grandparents' home in Connecticut. From your own experience, describe a cherished memory of a meal or pattern of eating together among your family or friends. Where were you? Who was there? What was your favorite food? Why is the memory so strong?

2. How do you eat meals today? Is a television set part of your family meal? What do you cherish and what do you regret about the meals you now share with others?

3. Consider the role of food in your congregation. When does your congregation eat together? What are some favorite occasions to share a common meal? What are some favorite foods at these congregational meals?

4. How do you experience Holy Communion? What adds to or subtracts from the experience for you?

Group Exercise

Plan a meal that your group will share with one another later in the week. Pick a day and time, and briefly plan the menu. No takeout foods are allowed!

Using the bread and the wine or grape juice your group leader brought, share Holy Communion in your small group, if doing so is acceptable in your tradition. Alternatively, your group can plan to prepare and offer Holy Communion to the whole congregation.

Weekly Reflection

Prepare a favorite meal for your family. In addition, plan a table blessing and ask everyone to share in the prayer. Consider inviting a guest to join you at your meal. What food did you prepare?

_____

_____

_____

_____

_____

_____

_____

_____

* * *

For further exploration, we invite you to read Chapter 3 in *Around the Fire*. The chapter discusses how the sharing of food can bond our families and human communities together. Various meanings of Holy Communion are explored, and a scene from the movie *Places in the Heart* is described to show how the Holy Meal can create a new community. We learn how the early church found its practice at mealtimes to be either supportive or destructive of community.

4.
What Happens When We Pray Together?

Prayer

Scripture Passages

They devoted themselves to ... prayer. (Acts 2:42a, c)

I thank my God every time I remember you. In all my prayers for all of you, I always pray with joy because of your partnership in the gospel from the first day until now, being confident of this, that he who began a good work in you will carry it on to completion until the day of Christ Jesus.

It is right for me to feel this way about all of you, since I have you in my heart and, whether I am in chains or defending and confirming the gospel, all of you share in God's grace with me. (Philippians 1:3-7)

Reflections and Comments

_____
_____
_____
_____
_____
_____
_____
_____
_____
_____
_____
_____
_____
_____

Signs of God's Presence

When you gather as a group, focus briefly on the lighted candle and on the cup and plate of Holy Communion. Touch the baptismal water in the bowl. Review your covenant agreement. Then focus on the posterboard with five concentric prayer circles.

Group Questions

1. When you were young, did your family ever pray together? If so, what was it like? How did it make you feel?

2. In the video, Rob describes the way a group of monks pray together on a regular schedule each day. Have you ever been part of a community where prayer was a regular and vital part of your routine? If not, do you wish you could experience such a community?

3. When Rob's mother was sick, he felt the support of a praying community, represented by the prayer shawl. Have you ever had an experience when you could feel other people praying for you or someone you love?

Group Exercise

Look at the posterboard with five concentric prayer circles. In the smallest circle in the middle, your small-group leader will write his or her name. In the next larger circle, the leader will write the first names of the members of your small group. In the next larger circle, the leader will write the names of a few people in your local congregation whom you feel need prayer. In the next-to-the-last circle, the leader will write the names of some people or issues in your local community that you feel need prayer. In the final and largest circle, the leader will write the names of some people or issues in the global community that you think could benefit from prayer. When you have finished, offer a prayer for the names and needs in each category, using the following model:

Name of God: Almighty God,

Attribute of God: who hears the prayers of all your children,

Petitions to God: hear us as we pray for... (Start with the smallest circle on your diagram and then expand your prayer requests by moving outward.)

Amen.

Your group may want to leave the posterboard of concentric circles on the wall so that participants can add to the list throughout the coming weeks.

Weekly Reflection

At home, create a diagram showing your own prayer circles. Use it to add to your intercessory prayers throughout the week. What or whom did you add?

_____
_____
_____
_____
_____
_____
_____
_____

* * *

For further exploration, we invite you to read Chapter 4 in *Around the Fire*. The chapter discusses how we can move from private prayer to prayer in community, using the stories of Paul in prison and Mark kneeling beside his mother before bed. A number of stories are shared that remind us of the power of prayer in community. We close by focusing on how to become more intentional about praying for other people.

5.
What's the Deal With Miracles?

Signs and Wonders

Scripture Passages

Everyone was filled with awe at the many signs and wonders performed by the apostles. (Acts 2:43)

In Lystra there sat a man who was lame. He had been that way from birth and had never walked. He listened to Paul as he was speaking. Paul looked directly at him, saw that he had faith to be healed and called out, "Stand up on your feet!" At that, the man jumped up and began to walk.

When the crowd saw what Paul had done, they shouted... "The gods have come down to us in human form!" Barnabas they called Zeus, and Paul they called Hermes because he was the chief speaker. The priest of Zeus, whose temple was just outside the city, brought bulls and wreaths to the city gates because he and the crowd wanted to offer sacrifices to them [Barnabas and Paul].

But when the apostles Barnabas and Paul heard of this, they tore their clothes and rushed out into the crowd, shouting: "Friends, why are you doing this? We too are only human, like you. We are bringing you good news, telling you to turn from these worthless things to the living God, who made heaven and earth and sea and everything in them." (Acts 14:8-15)

Reflections and Comments

_____

_____

_____

_____

_____
_____
_____
_____
_____
_____
_____
_____
_____
_____
_____
_____
_____

Signs of God's Presence

When you gather as a group, focus briefly on the lighted candle, the cup and plate of Holy Communion, your group's concentric prayer circles, and the baptismal water in the bowl. Then review your covenant agreement.

Group Questions

1. Have you seen or heard of a physical healing or other miraculous event that seemed supernatural? If so, describe what you saw.

2. In the video, Rob invites us to witness the work of God by recognizing where God is at work already. Rob points out that seeing the miraculous means choosing to awaken to wonder. Where do you see God evident in the natural world around you?

3. Where have you seen God's presence working through a community in ways that brought wholeness, healing, or forgiveness? Describe what you saw.

4. How do you respond when you pray for a miracle and nothing seems to happen?

Weekly Reflection

During the week, get a camera and take pictures of people, places, and events where you sense the presence of God at work. As you look through the photos you have taken, consider what God might be communicating through each one. Print out your pictures and bring some of them to class next week. List your pictures below:

_____

_____

_____

_____

_____

_____

_____

_____

* * *

For further exploration, we invite you to read Chapter 5 in *Around the Fire*. The chapter discusses how materialism and cynicism have clouded our eyes to God. It describes how the movie *Leap of Faith* illustrates the struggles of modern Christians to accept miracles. Why is it that some people see signs of God's work all around, while others do not? How can we rediscover the joy of seeing God's wonders all around us?

6.
What Do We Have in Common?

Stewardship

Scripture Passages

All who believed lived in close fellowship and possessed all things in common. They sold their belongings and property and gave their money to anyone who had need. (Acts 2:44-45, authors' paraphrase)

I thought it necessary to urge the brothers to visit you in advance and finish the arrangements for the generous gift you had promised. Then it will be ready as a generous gift, not as one grudgingly given.

Remember this: Whoever sows sparingly will also reap sparingly, and whoever sows generously will also reap generously. (2 Corinthians 9:5-6)

Reflections and Comments

_____

_____

_____

_____

_____

_____

_____

_____

_____

_____

_____

_____

_____

Signs of God's Presence

When you gather as a group, focus briefly on the lighted candle, the cup and plate of Holy Communion, your group's concentric prayer circles, and the baptismal water in the bowl. Then focus on an offering bowl or change purse as a sign of stewardship.

Group Questions

1. Describe a time in your life when someone gave of himself or herself to you in a powerful way. (The person might have been a family member, teacher, or church friend.) How has that gift shaped your life? How did it or might it encourage you to offer a similar gift to someone else?

2. Discuss the Xhosa African word *ubuntu*. (*Ubuntu* is a way of being community that includes mutuality and interdependence.) Do you find yourself yearning for *ubuntu*? Why or why not?

Group Exercise

Go around the circle and offer a talent, skill, or gift that you are willing to share with the other people in your small group. Reflect on the experience. How did it feel?

Your small-group leader will pass the offering plate or change purse around the circle. Each week you will have the opportunity to put money in the common offering. At the last session, the group will decide together where the money will go.

Weekly Reflection

Sometimes we fail to receive the gifts of others. What price have you paid in your life for times when you failed to receive gifts from other people?

_____

_____

_____

_____

_____

* * *

For further exploration, we invite you to read Chapter 6 in *Around the Fire*. The chapter begins with a description of the movie *Two Weeks Notice*, in which the lead character is possessed by his possessions. The chapter goes on to discuss how we can learn from the first Christians about sharing not only our possessions but also our lives with one another. The chapter ends with the story of "Stone Soup."

7.
How Can We Remember Who We Are?

Worship

Scripture Passage

Day by day, the followers of Jesus Christ spent much time together in the temple in Jerusalem. (Acts 2:46a, authors' paraphrase)

Reflections and Comments

_____

_____

_____

_____

_____

_____

_____

_____

_____

_____

_____

_____

_____

_____

_____

Signs of God's Presence

When you gather as a group, focus briefly on the lighted candle, the cup and plate of Holy Communion, your group's concentric prayer circles, and the baptismal water in the bowl. Then place an offering in the offering plate or change purse.

Group Questions

1. What is the most important anniversary in your life? How do you celebrate that anniversary? Why do you celebrate it?

2. In the video, Rob compares God's work in worship to that of a quilter. What does he mean?

3. Which aspect or act of worship means the most to you? Which act of worship means the least to you? Why?

4. Rob tells of a worship experience at a church in Harlem. Have you ever experienced God in worship in a way that changed your life? If so, when? Where? How did you respond?

Group Exercise

Go to worship this week and sit together with your small group.

With the other members of your group, plan and lead a worship service for your congregation. Visit with your pastor or worship leaders in advance to see how you might work together to accomplish this task.

Weekly Reflection

Spend some time preparing for worship next Sunday in your congregation. Pray for the worship service, the worship leaders, the other participants, and for your own participation in the service. If available, study the passage of Scripture that will be used for the sermon, read through the hymn or song texts, and read the prayers that will be used. What are you now expecting to happen in worship on Sunday?

_____

_____

_____

_____

_____

_____

_____

_____

* * *

For further exploration, we invite you to read Chapter 7 in *Around the Fire*. This chapter discusses how Andy once felt a profound sense of isolation from God and other people while sitting on top of Mount Sinai, where Moses received the Ten Commandments. In a culture that encourages isolation, this chapter explores how the church at worship helps us to rediscover and embrace God's mighty acts in history and in our own lives.

8.

How Can We Open Our Lives to Each Other?

Hospitality

Scripture Passages

They shared meals together from home to home.
> (Acts 2:46b, authors' paraphrase)

And let us consider how we may spur one another on toward love and good deeds, not giving up meeting together, as some are in the habit of doing, but encouraging one another. (Hebrews 10:24-25a)

Reflections and Comments

_____
_____
_____
_____
_____
_____
_____
_____
_____
_____
_____
_____
_____
_____
_____
_____
_____

Signs of God's Presence

When you gather as a group, focus briefly on the lighted candle, the cup and plate of Holy Communion, your group's concentric prayer circles, and the baptismal water in the bowl. Then place an offering in the offering plate or change purse.

Focus on the empty chair, a sign of hospitality.

Group Questions

1. Describe a recent occasion when you felt hospitality. It may have been at a restaurant, at a hotel, or in the home of a friend. Why was it a good experience? How did it make you feel?

2. Rob begins his talk by describing a circle of drummers, with one seat left open. Have you ever been welcomed into such a community? Have you experienced a church congregation such as this? If so, describe what it was like.

3. In the video, Rob describes the home in which he boarded in Germany and how it was arranged for conversation. What is the most important room in your home? Where does conversation take place in your home?

4. Who is missing from your congregation—not just those who are absent for a few weeks, but people who have never been a part of your congregation because of age, background, race, education, or economic situation? Why do you think these people have not attended? What would they add to your community? How might you invite them?

Weekly Reflection

Invite someone you would like to know better to eat with you this week: an older, single person in your congregation; a new resident in the area; a new coworker; a new family in your neighborhood. Reflect on the experience. Could such hospitality be a regular part of your life?

_____

_____

_____

_____

_____

_____

_____

_____

_____

* * *

For further exploration, we invite you to read Chapter 8 in *Around the Fire*. The chapter compares the friendship between characters in the old television show *I Love Lucy* with our modern culture of isolation. We encourage hospitality in the household of God, remembering that one of the first churches was built, literally, on the family home of Peter.

9.

How Can We Get Along
When We Are So Different?

Conflict Resolution

Scripture Passages

They ate their food with joy and thanksgiving, praising God and showing kindness to everyone. (Acts 2:46b-47a, authors' paraphrase)

Certain individuals came down from Judea to Antioch and were teaching the believers: "Unless you are circumcised, according to the custom taught by Moses, you cannot be saved." This brought Paul and Barnabas into sharp dispute and debate with them. So Paul and Barnabas were appointed, along with some other believers, to go up to Jerusalem to see the apostles and elders about this question. (Acts 15:1-2)

Reflections and Comments

_____
_____
_____
_____
_____
_____
_____
_____
_____
_____
_____
_____
_____
_____

Signs of God's Presence

When you gather as a group, focus briefly on the lighted candle, the cup and plate of Holy Communion, your group's concentric prayer circles, and the baptismal water in the bowl. Then place an offering in the offering plate or change purse and finish by focusing on the empty chair.

Group Exercise 1

Stand in a tight circle, with each person in the group facing the back of the person next to them, all facing the same direction. Bend your knees slowly until you are sitting on the knees of the person behind you, who is also bending his or her knees. After you succeed (or fail), reflect on the experience. What did you learn?

Group Questions

1. On a scale from one to ten, with ten being best, how do you rate yourself in dealing with conflict? How do you rate your congregation in dealing with conflict? Share your numbers with one another.

2. How did your family handle conflict when you were a child? What was your reaction to conflict? How did it affect you physically, emotionally, or spiritually? Do your childhood experiences still shape the way you deal with conflict today?

3. Consider John Wesley's rule for the small groups he created: "Do not speak ill of one another, and do not think ill of one another." Could this rule be valuable in your own congregation? Why?

4. Name a conflict in your local community or congregation. Without debating the pros and cons of the issue, where do you need some "glucosamine chondroitin" attitudes? What actions have made the problem worse? What actions could help resolve the conflict?

Group Exercise 2

Participate in the following roleplay. Try to resolve the conflict:

The members of Sweet Harmony Chapel all loved one another. Each week they worshiped together, prayed together, and shared a potluck lunch after church at 12:15 p.m. Many visitors, noticing this display of hospitality, joined the church.

Then, after ten years of leadership, Grandpa Hatfield decided to retire as chair of the board. Half of the members wanted Nephew Hatfield to be the new chair. He would ensure continuity with the past: The potluck lunch would start promptly at 12:15 p.m. every Sunday. Half of the members wanted a newcomer, Fresh McCoy, to be the new chair. He was committed to change: The lunch would begin at 12:45 p.m. The congregation began experiencing conflict and found themselves at an impasse.

Form two teams: the Hatfields and the McCoys. The Hatfields support the traditional time of lunch. The McCoys want to move lunch to a new time.

For five minutes, each team individually will prepare its case, naming its spokesperson and outlining its arguments. Then, with the small-group leader as moderator, each team will speak for five minutes.

How will you resolve the impasse?

Weekly Reflection

Name a person with whom you are in conflict. The conflict may be in the past or in the present. What ideas do you have for resolving the conflict? How could you be a catalyst in this process? Consider writing a brief letter to the person with whom you disagree.

Name a current conflict in your local congregation. Use the process described above to develop options for resolving the conflict. Consider sitting down with one or more of the other participants and sharing your observations.

Read Dr. Seuss's *The Butter Battle Book,* by A.S. Geisel (Random House, 1984). This book describes a long-running battle between the Yooks and the Zooks about which side of bread to butter.

To prepare for next week, reflect on all the characteristics of the body of Christ that we have discussed in this program: baptism, Holy Communion, prayer, signs and wonders, stewardship, worship, hospitality, and conflict resolution. Which of these characteristics are especially important to you? Which will you emphasize in the days to come? Be prepared to share your answers with your small group next week.

_____
_____
_____
_____
_____
_____
_____
_____
_____
_____
_____

* * *

For further exploration, we invite you to read Chapter 9 in *Around the Fire*. Because conflict is a natural part of life in community, the issue is not how to avoid conflict, but how to respond when it occurs. The movie *To Kill a Mockingbird* is cited as providing a wonderful illustration of conflict resolution. Some of Jesus' suggestions for resolving conflict are described; and the techniques used by a particular group of Christians, the Mennonites, are presented.

10.
How Do We Share What We Have Discovered?

Witness

Scripture Passages

And day by day, the Lord God increased the number of persons who were being saved. (Acts 2:47b, authors' paraphrase)

While Paul was waiting for them [Silas and Timothy] in Athens, he was greatly distressed to see that the city was full of idols. So he reasoned in the synagogue with both Jews and God-fearing Greeks, as well as in the market-place day by day with those who happened to be there. A group of Epicurean and Stoic philosophers began to debate with him. . . . Then they took him to a meeting of the Areopagus, where they said to him, "May we know what this new teaching is that you are presenting? You are bringing some strange ideas to our ears, and we would like to know what they mean." . . .

When they heard about the resurrection of the dead, some of them sneered, but others said, "We want to hear you again on this subject." At that, Paul left the Council. Some of the people became followers of Paul and believed.

(Acts 17:16-34)

Reflections and Comments

_____
_____
_____
_____
_____
_____
_____

Signs of God's Presence

When you gather as a group, focus briefly on the lighted candle, the cup and plate of Holy Communion, your group's concentric prayer circles, and the baptismal water in the bowl. Then place an offering in the offering plate or change purse and finish by focusing on the empty chair.

Group Questions

1. In the video, Rob describes how a church banquet was opened up to people who were "far away" but just around the corner. What are some ways your congregation can invite others in?

2. Discuss how your congregation welcomes guests. Are there ways in which your congregation could be more welcoming? What arc they?

3. Who introduced you to Jesus Christ? How old were you? Where were you? Who nurtured your faith? Divide into pairs and for five minutes describe your faith journey to your partner. Then listen to your partner tell his or her own story.

4. Think of a person—a neighbor, family member, or coworker—who might enjoy being a part of your church community. Why do you think they would benefit? How could you invite them? Will you invite them?

Group Exercise

Spend a few minutes deciding what to do with the money you have collected over the past few weeks. Designate a group member to carry out these wishes.

Choose one characteristic of community that you will observe in the days to come. Write down that characteristic on a slip of paper and place it on your refrigerator. Then let God guide you to develop the habit.

Offer a short blessing, handshake, or hug to the other people in your group.

Weekly Reflection

What brought you to this class? What has been your experience here? Review some highlights of *Longing to Belong*. What did you learn about yourself? What did you learn about the other people in your group? What did you learn about God? How have you been led to change? How will this experience change your life in your community of faith?

Set a date a month from now for a reunion and a discussion of next steps in being in community together.

_____
_____
_____
_____
_____
_____
_____
_____
_____
_____

* * *

For further exploration, we invite you to read Chapter 10 in *Around the Fire*. Several biblical models are explored for sharing experiences of God with family, neighbors, and friends. We may not desire to be "in-your-face" Christians, but what are some gracious options for telling people about God? We are reminded of a story from the television show *Seinfeld* that shows us how not to witness; we are invited instead to share our testimony with people who yearn to be part of a community where everyone knows their name.

What Next?

God lighted the fire of Pentecost. The flames of baptism, Communion, prayer, miracles, stewardship, worship, hospitality, and witness continue to light our way and heat our lives. How will we stoke the fire and let it spread?

Continuing to Be in Community

Through the past ten weeks, you have joined with other inquirers to ask some basic questions about how to live in community with other followers of Jesus Christ. In addition, you have learned how some Christians respond to those questions with regard to baptism, Holy Communion, prayer, signs and wonders, shared resources, worship, community, conflict resolution, and testimony. We pray that through these experiences you have found that you are not an island but a tree in the forest, with your roots entwined with many other trees. We hope that you have been caught up in the fiery passion of Pentecost.

Now is the time for you to consider how you will continue your spiritual journey. How will you risk finding community in your own life? What new behaviors will you adopt? Which old attitudes will you discard? Where will you go now that the study is over?

Begin by celebrating what you have already accomplished! Through your participation in the study you have demonstrated a steadfast effort to ask serious questions, engage in deep dialogue, and learn from other people who are also on a journey with God. You have begun to experience a part of the community called the church. On this journey, however, be aware that you may never arrive at a final destination. You and your group are making progress toward becoming the person and the loving community God created all of us to be.

We invite you to risk choosing to live a full, abundant, loving, and never-ending life with Jesus Christ in community with other people. Who does not wish to have such a life? Why would we choose to live a life that diminishes us, takes us down the wrong road, or leads us in the opposite direction from where we hope to be? Our society encourages us to be islands and live alone. Jesus Christ offers us the presence of God and other believers. Each of us has a choice. Now is the time for you to help create such a community where you live today.

"Be united with other Christians. A wall with loose bricks is not good. The bricks must be cemented together."[1]

Corrie ten Boom

One important way to continue your growth in Jesus Christ is to remain connected with the people from your small group or class. You may have found some new friends and wish to continue those relationships. Your group may decide to remain together as a weekly Bible study group or Sunday school class. You might consider using the second study in the *Beginnings* series, *The Spiritual Life*. We anticipate that there will be a fourth study, *Sharing the New Creation*. We encourage you to sponsor a reunion of your small group a week or so after your class concludes for a supper or lunch meeting. See who comes, and make some plans together. The goal will be to encourage one another to grow together.

We especially urge you to consider bringing someone to the next session of *Beginnings: An Introduction to Christian Faith*. This first study in the *Beginnings* series introduces seekers and inquirers to the basic beliefs of Christianity by asking some questions: Who was Jesus Christ? What is the Bible? How do we pray? Why should we be a part of a community of believers?

Of course, the journey toward serious Christian discipleship is bigger than any study or series. We believe that active participation in the life of a Christian congregation is a critical part of the journey. The nurturing of your life in that community will take time and care, as you receive the ongoing guidance of the Spirit of God.

However you decide to continue your journey, please do so with intentionality, knowing that Jesus Christ through the Spirit is with you and your community in the journey toward wholeness. As basketball coach Mike Krzyzewski once wrote:

> You should live the journey.
> You should live it right.
> You should live it together.
> You should live it shared.
> You should try to make one another better.
> You should get on one another if somebody's
>   not doing their part.
> You should hug one another when they are....
> It's all about the journey....
> Let's go.[2]

1. Corrie ten Boom quoted in *Fuel for the Journey*, by Lowell McNaney and Andy Lambert (Whitaker Ink, 2003); page 54.
2. FROM LEADING WITH THE HEART, by MIKE KRZYZEWSKI. Copyright © 2000 by Mike Krzyzewski. Foreword © 2000 by Grant Hill. By permission of Grand Central Publishing.